Criminal Defense

Contents

Introduction

Domestic violence refers to one partner in a marital or romantic/intimate relationship being abused by the other partner. It is one of the most terrible and significant social dilemmas recognized by non-governmental and governmental agencies. Normally, in a relationship, women are subjected to domestic violence more frequently than men are; however, it doesn't mean that the male gender does not undergo any harm or pain due to this issue.

In recent times, more men than women are being victimized by domestic violence. In the U.S., around 3.2 million men and 1.9 million women are physically abused every year and around 7.4 percent men and about 22.1 percent women undergo domestic violence inflicted by their ex-spouse, girlfriend/boyfriend, cohabiting partner or a date. These statistics correspond to the data pertinent to domestic violence collected in 2000.

According to a NISVS survey carried out in 2001, it was discovered that around 21.6 percent of male domestic violence victims were threatened by their female counterparts with a dagger or knife, which is far more than the 12.7 percent of female victims who were threatened in a similar manner.

Another NISVS survey in 2011 reported that 41.7 percent victims of harsh physical abuse were men. Around 4,741,000 women were subjected to physical abuse in the past year, of which 66.7 percent were beaten harshly and about 4.3 percent of the male victims were treated in a similar manner. Although this number of male victims is smaller compared to that of women, it is still quite significant compared to that during the 1980s and 1990s.

The ever-increasing problem of domestic violence is due to the lack of education and comprehension of the rights of an individual in a relationship. This is exactly why this book has been compiled: to educate people about the nature of domestic violence, reasons of its prevalence and measures that must be taken to control this issue.

The first chapter walks you through is the definition of domestic violence and everything that this subject encompasses. You will find out the acts that are included in domestic violence and those that must not be construed as domestic violence. It also informs you about the consequences you would have to bear if you back someone who is a victim of domestic violence. In addition to that, you would also find out some of the common domestic violence crimes, consequences of defending an innocent person in a domestic violence crime and resulting scenarios if you had decided to support someone who wasn't innocent.

Moving on to the second chapter, you would be educated about the technicalities involved in a domestic violence case. You would find out what you need to do when a domestic violence case takes place. What should a victim do? Should they press charges or not? These are few of the questions that will be answered in this part.

Moreover, you'd find out who can be termed as a victim: what are the characteristics of a person victimized by sexual or physical abuse, what problems do victims experience, and how and why a victim can refuse to testimony for this crime. Secondly, you would find out what questions you need to ask a person to confirm that they were subjected to domestic violence, what importance does asking the right questions have and what can happen if you forget to ask a significant question. You would also find out what problems do immigrants subjected to this problem face and the penalties imposed by the State of

California on the criminals involved in a domestic violence case. Finally, the book will be concluded by laying emphasis on the significant points of the topic.

The knowledge exhibited in this book would be able to equip you with all the information you need for defending a victim in a domestic violence case and for educating people about their rights.

Chapter 1 - Understanding Domestic Violence

What is Domestic Violence?

According to sub-chapter III of chapter 136, title 42 of the U.S. Code, domestic violence comprises misdemeanor crimes or felonies of violence committed by the existing or ex-spouse of the person victimized by this act, by the one who shares a biological child with the victim, by the one who was in a cohabiting relationship with the one who was victimized, by the one who is considered as the victim's spouse, or by anybody who has been restrained by law to victimize any person.

This excerpt was also incorporated in the 'Violence Against Women Act of 1994', by the section 3a, included in the Violence Against Women and Department of Justice Reauthorization Act of 2005. It is also applicable for purposes in section 775 in subpart 17 of the part D in chapter V of chapter 70, title 20 and the section 1437F of subchapter I in chapter 8 in title 42, as well as the subchapter XII-H of chapter 46 of title 42 of the U.S. Code.

The OVW (Office on Violence Against Women) of the U.S. has defined domestic violence as an abusive behavior that exists in any intimate relationship and is exercised by one of the two partners in the relationship for gaining or maintaining power, as well as control over the other partner. According to the definition, domestic violence or acts involving physical and sexual abuse can take place with anyone irrespective of their age, race, religion, gender and sexual orientation and it can take several forms, such as sexual, verbal, economic, physical, psychological and emotional abuse.

The basic purpose of all the types of domestic violence is to gain as well as maintain complete control over the victim. It gives the assaulter a certain sense of satisfaction and empowerment. The abusers exercise various tactics of exerting power over their victim who can be their partner, spouse or just a date. Some of these tactics include intimidation, blame, denial, threats, isolation and humiliation. The dynamics of domestic violence can include any or all of the following:

- Situational Couple Domestic Violence: It occurs due to conflicts that quickly turn into violent arguments and are converted to violence. It is not normally associated with a control pattern and is the most commonly occurring form of intimate partner domestic violence. Both the genders can be the abusers in this form. However, women normally incur more physical harm than men do.

- Intimate Terrorism: It encompasses an ongoing control pattern that uses physical, emotional and several other kinds of domestic abuse and violence. Women are more frequently victimized by this type of violence. The definition of intimate terrorism was the initial definition of domestic violence as well, and it is normally exhibited by using the 'Power and Control Wheel' for illustrating the various inter-related kinds of abuse.

- Common Couple Violence: In this form, both the partners are involved in inflicting domestic violence on one another.

- MVC: MVC or mutual violent control is a very uncommon form of intimate partner/spouse violence that takes place when both the partners in the relationship act with each other violently in order to gain complete control over the other.

- Controlling Behavior: This behavior basically encompasses several acts that are used for making one person in the relationship the subordinate of or completely dependent on the other person. This is done mostly by cutting them off completely from all resources of financial aid and support, exploiting all their resources or capacities for their personal gain, divesting them of all the means that are required for resistance, independence and escape, as well as regulating routine behavior.

- Coercive Behavior: It is either just one act or a range of several acts of threats, assault, intimidation or any other abuse that is exercised for punishing, frightening or harming their victim.

- Economic Domestic Violence: When you have money and are in a position to take decisions regarding it, but do not give your spouse control over it and make them financially dependent you are imposing economic domestic violence on them.

- Spiritual Violence: If you don't allow your partner or spouse to have opinions regarding cultural beliefs, values and religion and manipulate their spirituality, it is known as spiritual violence.

These were the common types of domestic violence and if anyone has been involved in relationships where their partner practiced any of these types with them, they were victimized by this heinous act. In addition to that, you should know the different situations where you tend to become violent, but aren't viewed as domestic violators in the eyes of law.

- Self Defense: If you are trying to resist the violent acts of your partner and act violently with them in order to defend yourself against the harms they are inflicting on you, then you won't be guilty of this crime, rather you would be seen as the victim. This is also referred to as 'violent resistance'. It means that you believed or knew that you were going to suffer from extreme harm or injuries and realized that the instant use of a violent act or force was the only option left to safeguard yourself from that harm. Furthermore, you made use of the precise amount of force that was necessary for keeping you safe and you did not resort to an unnecessarily extreme measure of force. If your spouse or partner attacked you severely and you reacted to their violence in a harsh manner just to protect yourself, then you won't be charged with domestic violence.

- Not a Parent, Cohabitant or Spouse: If you were violent with someone, but are not the parent of that person's children, nor their former spouse, current spouse, cohabiting partner or former cohabitant, then you won't be convicted of domestic violence; however, you might be charged with other crimes like assault using a harmful weapon or criminal battery.

- No Traumatic State: If no injuries have been reported when you were arrested for domestic violence, then you can use that in your defense and are most likely to escape being convicted with this charge. Even if there are a few minor injuries, then too, there is a good chance you won't be guilty of domestic violence because minor injuries are normally not viewed as domestic violence and you can use this point as leverage for reducing your charges.

Understanding the Symptoms of Domestic Violence

Let's take a look at the different signs and symptoms of domestic violence that signify an act of domestic violence.

- Disrespect: This includes putting the victim down or lowering their morale in front of others, not listening to them when they talk to you, interrupting their telephone calls, forcefully taking money from their purse without getting their permission and refusing to help them with housework or childcare.

- Verbal Abuse and Destructive Criticism: These are all those different acts that are used for verbally abusing a person to inflict destructive harm on their personality. It includes mocking, accusing, shouting, name-calling and verbal threatening.

- Pressure Tactics: These include the different acts that are used for pressurizing the victim. These include threatening to withhold money, sulking, disconnecting the telephone, taking the car or any other vehicle away, trying to commit suicide, taking kids away, reporting to the welfare agencies until you obey their demands regarding nurturing the kids, lying to family and friends and telling them that you don't have any choice in making a decision.

- Isolation: This includes blocking or monitoring their telephone calls, telling them where they should or shouldn't go, preventing them from visiting their relatives and friends.

- Breaking Faith/Trust: This comprises lying to your partner/spouse, keeping important information from them getting jealous for no significant reason, betraying their trust and resorting to infidelity and breaking promises.

- Harassment: This includes following them, checking on them, opening their mail, frequently checking who has called, mailed or telephoned them and embarrassing them in public.

- Sexual Violence: It includes making use of force, intimidation or threats for making the victim perform romantic or sexual acts or to have sex with you at a time when they don't want it.

- Threats: This includes making angry and violent gestures, making use of physical size and physique for intimidating them, shouting at the victim, destroying their possessions, punching walls, breaking things, threatening to harm or kill them and the kids and wielding a gun or a knife.

- Denial: This involves saying that the abuse did not take place and acting as the innocent person, crying or being gentle, begging to the victim in front of the public and asking for their forgiveness.

- Physical Violence: This includes hitting, kicking, slapping, punching, biting, pushing, pinching, burning, shoving, strangling and pulling their hair out.

What is Not Domestic Violence?

Domestic violence is quite a huge subject and now you are aware of everything that is termed as domestic violence. However, there are certain acts that are violent in nature, but are not construed as acts of domestic violence. There exists a fine line between violence and domestic violence and it is important that you comprehend that difference, so you know when you need to press charges for domestic violence and when you must not.

Take a look at all the incidents that are not termed as domestic violence.

- A boyfriend or girlfriend screaming or yelling at the other, or one spouse screaming at the other

- Using profanity in an argument with your spouse, girlfriend/boyfriend or member of the household

- Engaging in minor acts of pushing your spouse, girlfriend/boyfriend or member of the household

- Engaging in a consensual act of sex or sex that is rough or loud

- Engaging in wrestling matches, pillow fights or horseplay with your girlfriend/boyfriend, spouse or member of the household

- Holding your girlfriend's/boyfriend's, spouse's, or household member's arm or hand during an argument

- Restraining your intimate partner to stop them from harming themselves or any other family member

- Blocking your girlfriend's/boyfriend's, spouse's or household member's path momentarily

- Throwing and breaking items while fighting or engaging in sexual acts

- Waking up violently while seeing a nightmare

- Reacting violently when somebody wakes you up suddenly

- Saying hurtful, mean or disrespectful things to your girlfriend/boyfriend, household member or spouse

- Using self-defense to stop your boyfriend/girlfriend, household member or spouse from harming you physically

- Fighting for your rights in a heated argument

- Unintentionally pushing your girlfriend/boyfriend, household member or spouse in an argument

- One-time threat to leave your partner or spouse

- One-time threat to stop speaking to your partner or to stop supporting them

In addition to that, it is also important that you understand the different myths related to domestic violence. Having complete comprehension of these myths, will help you gain a better understanding of this subject.

- Domestic violence normally affects the population's tiny amount: Most people are of the opinion that domestic violence only affects a tiny portion of the country's or the world's population and does not take place very often. However, this is completely untrue. According to the national researches that have been conducted in the past, it has been concluded that around three to four million women are subjected to beatings every year. In a study executed in 1995, it was found out that about 31 percent of the women surveyed in the study were subjected to brutal physical assaults by their boyfriend or husband. Domestic violence was also discovered as the main reason of injuries of women belonging to the age group of 15 to 44. According to the FBI, one woman gets beaten in every 15-20 seconds in the country and 30 percent of the victims in female homicide cases are murdered by their ex-partners or current partners. Furthermore, around 1,500 women are murdered in domestic violence cases taking place in the U.S. every year.

- Women can be as brutal as their male counterparts are: People, who do not view domestic violence as a big crime or problem, often argue that women tend to be as violent and brutal as their male counterparts are. In a study carried out by the competent Dr. Murray Strauss, working at the University of New Hampshire, it was discovered that women often use violent measures for resolving conflicts and arguments in relationships, just like men do. The research also exhibited that, after measuring the consequences and contexts of different assault cases, it was observed that women were victimized in most of those cases. The Department of Justice in U.S. discovered that 85 percent of victims subjected to spousal abuse and assault are women. Men are victims too, but this case is quite rare.

- Alcohol abuse results in domestic violence: There exists a strong correlation between substance abuse or alcohol and battering, but this relationship isn't a causal one. Batterers do drink and use their drinking as an excuse for their violent acts, so they can place the entire responsibility of their heinous act on the intoxication caused by alcohol. You need to be clear about one thing, which alcohol abuse does not always result in domestic violence. Quitting drinking or substance abuse does not mean that, that person will put an end to their violent measures. Substance abuse and battering must be addressed as separate issues and should not overlap individual problems and need to be tackled separately.

- Pregnant women are not subjected to domestic violence: This is an entirely wrong concept. According to the national surveys, it has been observed that around 5.3 percent of the pregnant women face domestic violence every year. This means about 324,000 women face violence by their intimate partner, while they are expecting a child.

- Women belonging to the middle class don't get beaten as often as women belonging to the poor class: No, this statement is yet again a common myth related to domestic violence. Domestic violence takes place in every socio-economic group, be it an elite class or the lower class. Middle class women frequently suffer from domestic violence and go through countless hurdles when they try to get help for their situation. There are many men from the elite class, who have studied in the finest educational institutions, yet they love to harass their female counterparts for the sake of satisfying their underlying hunger for power and control.

- Abusers use violence in every relationship they are involved in: No, every batterer does not use violence in every relationship they are involved in. Normally, they resort to violent acts in their intimate relationships only, and their non-intimate relationships stay safe from their violent side.

- Batterers get violent because they unintentionally lost their anger: Batterers resort to violence as it assists them in gaining control and power over their victim and it has nothing to do with their temper. It is a built-in condition in their mind.

- The victim asked for violence: Nobody wants to be beaten or battered, so stating that the victim asked for a violent measure or practiced an act that provoked that act of violence is absolutely wrong. An abuser will seldom accept that they purposefully indulged in the violent act and are indeed its cause. Placing the entire blame for that act on the innocent victim is actually a strategy to manipulate them and the others around them. Batterers stating that 'the victim aggravated their temper or made them jealous' is actually a measure to shift their burden on the victim.

- Domestic violence isn't a serious problem like street crimes and other criminal acts: No, domestic violence is as bad and heinous as any other crime and acts of this nature make a home an unsafe place for the victim. One's home is supposed to be a place where one can seek refuge from everything bad and evil. However, when one is subjected to terror and violence in their own home, they don't have anywhere else to go for comfort. Domestic violence is indeed the reason for the onset of several other crimes such as rape, homicide and aggravated assault.

- Domestic violence and abuse is a wife and husband's personal matter: People who want to turn a blind eye to this issue often state that domestic abuse is a personal matter between two people in a relationship, be it a husband and wife, two cohabiting partners, or a girlfriend and boyfriend. No, domestic violence casts a certain effect on everyone. One in every three American women has been subjected to sexual or physical abuse sometime in her life, by her partner or spouse. In 1996, around 30 percent of all the female victims in murder cases were murdered by their boyfriends or husbands. Around 40 to 60 percent men who inflict harm on women also harm and abuse children.

- Men who are violent with their wives/partners are good fathers: Studies have revealed that men who frequently batter their spouses/partners or girlfriends also abuse their own kids in around 70 percent of the domestic violence cases. Even if children aren't directly subjected to violence, they do suffer a lot emotionally, when they witness one of their parents assaulting the other. Batterers normally show a great interest in maintaining contact with their kids when they are separated, so they can get in touch with their separated spouse/partner again and gain control over them once more.

- All the household members of a family, in which domestic violence is taking place, should try to stop the violence: Yes, the members of the family can try to stop the violence, but only the one inflicting harm on the other has the ultimate right to put an end to that violence. Battering and beating is indeed a behavioral option that the batterer selects and only they should be held responsible and accountable for it. Most battered women try changing their own behavior for the reason that their attempt might put an end to the abuse, but this doesn't really work.

- Beaten women are mainly masochistic: Even if battered women have a masochistic approach, it does not mean they should be treated with abuse or disrespect. When a woman is victimized, she makes several attempts of leaving the relationship, but is prevented from achieving her goal by the abuser, as he tries to increase the intensity and amount of violence on her. In addition to that, other issues that inhibit her ability to get out of the relationship include support, housing, economic independence, social isolation, religious or cultural constraints and a commitment made to the batterer. Moreover, a study concluded that the danger imposed on the victim boosts by a staggering 70 percent when she tries to get out of the relationship.

- Men have the responsibility to discipline and control their partners when they misbehave: Battering must never be viewed as a measure to discipline or order somebody, be the violator a man or a woman. Our society has its roots in a legal patriarchal system that has given men the legal right to reprimand their kids and wives physically. However, this system is no longer prevalent. Children and women aren't considered as a man's property anymore, which is why they don't have the right to inflict violence on them.

- Domestic violence and abuse is an isolated occurrence: Battering is often termed as an isolated occurrence that won't take place again. However, one must understand that beating isn't one physical assault. It encompasses the frequent use of several tactics such as threats, isolation, economic deprivation, sexual abuse, psychological abuse and intimidation.

Now that you have gone through these myths, you can better understand that domestic violence must not be viewed as a reason or as an attempt to protect yourself from something. It is a crime and must be treated as one too.

The Consequences

In most situations, someone is charged with domestic violence after an argument between the spouses gets out of hand. Both parties clearly did not intend for it to happen, but before they know it, the police are knocking on their door. In most cases, the police arrests one of the parties based on the statement the other made in anger. This is their strategy to defuse the situation. The person is arrested on the charges of "inflicting corporal injury" on their partner or cohabitant, or they might also be charged with the less serious offense of "criminal spousal battery".

The other spouse is usually left in a quandary as his or her partner is currently in jail and there is required a considerable amount of money for bail. The bail amount is normally between the sums of 20 and 50 thousand dollars or even higher. The aforementioned spouse could also be facing charges, which could precede a severe penalty or penalties. All this is the outcome of a petty misunderstanding, where one person made some statements in an emotional state, which could possibly be inaccurate. Now that the consequences are clear, the person is going to have a felony charge on their permanent criminal record and would have to be bailed out; the family is in turmoil and has to suffer for what may have been a small argument.

How Lawyers Can Help

When the situation that has been described above occurs, the parties involved are ready to take any measures to free their family member and put an end to the whole story. To achieve this, they contact the police and make statements to cover up their previous ones because it is their belief that the police also want to settle the matter and close the case by finding out the real story. They are, however, completely wrong! Making further statements and calling the police again will only aggravate the situation and put the person in a worse situation. The family should not contact the police under any circumstances!

In such a scenario, the only person the family can trust is their lawyer. The lawyer should have experience in criminal cases. Often in such cases of domestic violence as that mentioned above, or much more complicated ones, are resolved with the accused party walking away without a penalty. If handled with tact and expertise, many defenses as well as defense strategies may be used by a lawyer who is familiar with them. It could result in the defendant being declared innocent.

Possible Charges for Domestic Violence

Criminal charges of spousal abuse made against a person, which involved domestic violence, can lead to two usual charges that the person might face in a criminal court of the State of California. The charges are corporal injury inflicted on a spouse, which is categorized as a felony or the standard case of misdemeanor known as spousal battery. Many issues can arise out of such criminal cases, which are a culmination of domestic violence.

It is crucial to know that every case is different from other cases of domestic violence, but an experienced lawyer who is familiar with all the facts and details of the case can give legitimate advice and help resolve the criminal matter smoothly. This is why families going through such an ordeal immediately hire the right person for the job; they hire a person who can help their loved one avoid any criminal charges.

Corporal Injury Inflicted on the Spouse or a Cohabitant

A charge of corporal injury inflicted on the spouse or a cohabitant can be made against a person, if the said person has willfully inflicted corporal injury on their spouse, cohabitant, former spouse, former cohabitant, or any person who is the birth parent of their child. The injury must lead to a serious traumatic condition of the person.

For such a crime, the attorney needs to provide proof that the person who has been charged with the crime of corporal injury inflicted on the spouse or a cohabitant, only intended to commit the physical act. The fact that the person was intent on injuring the person because of the act should not be mentioned or insinuated.

According to the California State Penal code, "traumatic condition" is a term used to define the condition a body is in after it has been wounded or injured. It does not matter how serious or severe the injury or wound is. Even a light bruise would constitute as a "traumatic condition" and the case would be filed under the criminal charges of corporal injury inflicted on the spouse or a cohabitant. However, the injury has to be physical and emotional distress or a mild ache will not count.

It is important to note that, when the police are alerted of an incident of domestic violence, if there happens to be an injured party, regardless of how minor the injury is, the police is bound by the law to arrest the other party based on criminal conduct.

Punishment

The penalties stated below are as dictated by California's own penal code. A lawyer can get a much more lenient sentence for you.

The penalty for hitting your spouse and injuring them is punishable with an imprisonment sentence of two to four years, or a year or less in a county jail and being dealt a heavy fine.

If someone is convicted for battery of a spouse on more than instance, then that person can only be tried and sentenced for one offence and the other instances are stayed.

If a person has a record of domestic abuse of a spouse or a cohabitant, and the previous offense has occurred within 7 years, the punishment they face might be more severe depending on their previous criminal record.

If a spouse or cohabitant is hit and injured during the time the first crime has been charged and is being tried, the sentence can be increased to an extra time in prison, which will make the sentence at least 3 to 5 years.

Battery of the Spouse or a Cohabitant

Unlike the criminal offense discussed above, battery of the spouse or a cohabitant does not come with a very strict and worrying punishment; nonetheless, it is not a simple matter. According to the California State Penal code, battery is defined as any use of violence or force that is willful as well as unlawful, upon another person.

When a person is accused of battery against their spouse or their cohabitant, or the birth parent of their child, their fiancée, former spouse or any such individual who has been in a relationship or in engagement with them then that person may on account of the California State Penal code be charged with the crime of battery of the spouse or a cohabitant.

This case is quite opposite to that of a corporal injury inflicted on the spouse or a cohabitant; here no evidence of an injury is required to report the crime. Therefore, the victim of the crime of spousal battery may file criminal charges, even if they are completely fine.

In some cases, even if there is a physical injury because of the domestic violence, a criminal lawyer who is experienced in such cases, can successfully negotiate and bring down the felony charge to the less serious misdemeanor of battery of the spouse or a cohabitant. This is why families make sure they have hired the best person to represent them, when they are facing such charges.

Punishment

The punishment for domestic battery of a spouse or cohabitant results in a fine along with a jail sentence of a year or less (at times, it is either one of the two).

In some cases of alleged domestic violence against a spouse, we have successfully gotten our clients off with only a minimal fine and no jail time!

Probation for Crimes of Domestic Violence

In many cases, an experienced lawyer can work out a plea bargain with a judge that will not make their client do any jail time for his charge of domestic violence. As a result, the client can be ordered to attend sessions for anger management or something of the sort and no jail sentence has to be served, but this only happens when a client agrees to plead guilty for his crime.

If you or someone you know has been arrested or detained for domestic violence in California, then a suitable lawyer must represent him/her. This case is tried in a criminal court and only a lawyer with ample experience in practicing criminal law can sufficiently help you.

California's Law on "Felon with a Firearm"

The penal code 29800 is known as the "felon with firearm" law in California. This law makes it a criminal offence to carry a gun after you have been convicted of a felony. This means if you have been arrested and tried for domestic violence and had a gun in your possession at the time, you are prohibited for the rest of your life to own and possess a gun in California.

Violation of the code is faced with a penalty:

1 year and 4 months, or two to three years in the state prison of California or a fine of $10,000 maximum.

The Penal Code 29805 is California's 10-year prohibition of firearms.

Under this code, there are around forty misdemeanor offences, which allow for a ten-year prohibition of firearms.

This list includes physical battery, verbal threats and stalking people on multiple instances.

If you have ever been or are convicted of domestic violence, under the California law, you are banned from carrying a gun for ten years! However, after the ten years are over, you can possess a gun without any worries or procedures. This may be revoked, however, if you had anywhere in the ten-year ban, had another firearms ban invoked on yourself.

18 United States Code 922(g) is the firearms ban by the federal government.

The California state law may allow for a ten-year ban, but the federal law dictates that those convicted of domestic violence shall have a lifetime ban on possessing firearms. Furthermore, if a case arises where federal and the California laws dispute each other, the federal law will always take precedence.

Many of the people convicted of domestic violence in California, will not be able to possess a gun anywhere else in the country as well.

If you do happen to possess a gun, which is directly violating federal law, you are in danger of being charged a fine of up to $250,000! That is not all; you may also have to serve ten years or less in a federal prison!

Domestic Violence is Grounds for Deportability of Immigrants

If you are a non-citizen and have been convicted of domestic violence, stalking, child neglect or abuse and abandoning a child after September 30 1996, you may be deported! This has been permitted by the section 237, under the Immigration and Nationality act. Even if the person holds a visa or a green card, they are still viable to be deported for the crimes stated above.

This means that if a current or a former spouse, co-parent or live-in partner or ex-spouse who commits domestic violence against someone who is protected under the state or federal law is committing domestic violence.

Common Domestic Violence Crimes

The state of California realizes domestic violence offenses in several familial and intimate relationship scenarios. These criminal offenses are in relation to a California Penal Code that specifies a domestic violence crime against a current or former spouse, a current or a former cohabitant, a parent with whom he or she bears a child, or a partner whom the individual is dating.

Once a prosecutor has to defer the kind of domestic violence charge that suitably applies to an individual, the prosecutor, based on the severity and scenario, assesses numerous Penal Codes. By evaluating the extent of harm done to an individual and on the type of condition, the prosecutor takes a fact-based decision on the kind of Penal Code associated with domestic violence crime that is applicable on the individual.

Penal Code 273.5 pc Corporal Injury to a Spouse or Cohabitant

"Penal Code 273.5 makes it illegal to inflict a "corporal injury" resulting in a "traumatic condition." A person commits this crime by striking his/her intimate partner in some violent way and causing a visible injury, even a slight one such as swelling or a bruise. This California domestic violence law can be charged if the alleged victim is a current or former spouse or cohabitant or the parent of your child."

According to this Penal Code, the accuser can apply for a misdemeanor or a felony charge on an individual who is guilty of battery, spousal abuse, corporate injury, domestic abuse or domestic violence. Once the accuser has charged an individual with this kind of domestic violence charge, the penalties are inflicted upon the accused once the investigation starts and cannot be dropped in any case, even when the accuser decides later to reverse his or her statements or willfully drop the case. Unlike other laws, the charges of domestic violence crimes cannot be dropped and the accused will have to undergo penalties whichever they may be. The specified Penal Code is applicable to the smallest of injuries that are caused during any type of the specified domestic violence crimes. The investigating team will take photographs in such cases and then it is inevitable to reverse the charges, once this kind of evidence is gained.

The penalties for a misdemeanor violation, includes the following:

- Three years of informal probation
- A year in the county jail
- Up to $6,000 fines
- Scheduled payments to battered women organizations
- Scheduled payments to the alleged victim
- A protective order
- A restraining order
- A year's worth of abuse classes
- Counseling services
- Community service

The penalties for a felony violation, includes the following:

- Formal probation
- Four years in prison
- Five additional years for inflicting "great bodily injury"
- Payments, orders, abuse classes, community service, and counseling

Penal Code 243(e) (1) pc Domestic Battery

"Penal Code 243(e)(1) makes it a misdemeanor crime to inflict force or violence on an intimate partner...a category that includes your fiancé, cohabitant, the parent of your child, or your current or former spouse or dating partner. Unlike Penal Code 273.5, this California domestic violence law does not require a visible injury."

Under the specified California Law Penal Code, misdemeanor charges are issued on a partner or spouse who is accused of applying willful domestic abuse to the intimate partner in terms of force or abuse. This is the most general kind of domestic violence charges and it is applicable to all kinds of relationship scenarios, including those of both a homosexual and a heterosexual relationship.

This Penal Code for domestic violence is applicable to the defendant who is proven guilty after all related court proceedings. This kind of Penal Code is different from others, in a way that a misdemeanor charge can be issued to the accused even if no physical injury is inflicted on the victim. With that, if investigators have evidence of a physical injury, then serious Penal Codes are applied. Moreover, violence or force is more commonly confused with the emergence of a physical injury. In case of a misdemeanor charge for this Penal Code, pushing your partner by using force can also indulge that individual in the specified allegations.

To specify an intimate partner legally, a spouse, fiancé, mother or father of your child and the person you were previously or are currently dating are all taken under consideration. In addition, this Penal Code of domestic violence is applicable in terms of the scenario in which the intimate partner has developed a contact with the accuser, such as with his or her body, clothing, or anything else that may result in connecting with him or her in a way.

A misdemeanor charge is applied on an individual who has been accused with this Penal Code and that individual may suffer the following charges:

- One year in jail

- $2,000 fine

- Informal probation for up to three years

- To complete a batterer's program

- Pay money to women's shelters and the alleged victim for legal costs

- Therapy

- Other expenses arising from your alleged incident

With that, there are possible defense strategies that can be used to waive off the misdemeanor charges associated with the specified Penal Code of domestic violence crime. For that, if the defendant manages to prove that he or she has been wrongly accused, has acted in that way as a means of self-defense, or the incident took place as an accident, this Penal Code may not apply to them since it requires a "willful" action of domestic violence.

Penal Code 273d pc Child Abuse

"Penal Code 273d makes it a crime to inflict "corporal punishment or injury" on a child if it was "cruel or inhuman" and caused an injury (even a slight injury). California child abuse laws allow a parent reasonable latitude to spank a child, but draw the line where the punishment is cruel or injures the child."

With being a parent, comes very high expectations in terms of societal pressure and those from your child too. The best way to groom your child is by forming an effective and honest communication with him or her. Since most parents are working, children may feel neglected or stressed out, if they are not getting adequate attention that they think they deserve. In such a case, the parents may react harshly and lead to disrupted parent-child relationships. In California, the laws related to child abuse are strict and they happen to limit the ways adopted by parents to groom their child. With that, these laws ensure maximum security for your child.

According to the specified Penal Code of domestic violence, if a parent inflicts physical injury or abuse over his or her child as a means of punishment, or to refrain the child from adopting a dangerous action, then the parent is in serious trouble and will be charged as a convict. The accused may also have to suffer jail time for using "physical violence" against the child. Emotional violence is ruled out in this kind of Penal Code and it is referred to in another law.

The following are generally considered acts of physical abuse on your child, according to the specified Penal Code and the accuser will suffer serious criminal convictions for it:

- Hitting a child in a way that leaves a mark

- Fighting physically with your child leaving marks and/or bruises

- Using a belt to beat a child in an attempt to discipline him/her

With that, if you think your child is wrongly accusing you of domestic violence, there are ways in which you can turn the criminal convictions away and get a favorable statement from the court. With so many laws that restrict the way in which you groom your child, many miscommunications follow. Teenagers, going through an array of emotions and resentment at this tender age, are more likely to press charges on their parents, which may or may not apply to them. To avoid charges in a case where you believe you are being wrongly accused, discuss it with your attorney. The attorney will look into the evidence with critical analysis to determine whether the Penal Code for child abuse applies to the parent or not.

In case a parent is charged with a misdemeanor for violating child abuse laws of this Penal Code

- One year in jail

In case a parent is charged with a Felony for violating child abuse laws of this Penal Code

- Six years in prison

In case, a parent has a previous history of child abuse and is accused with this Penal Code

- More than six years in prison

Penal Code 273a pc Child Endangerment

"Penal Code 273a makes it a crime willfully to allow a child (in your care or custody) to suffer harm or to have his/her safety or health endangered. An example would be a mother who permits her boyfriend to beat her 6-year-old; or a parent who operates a dangerous meth lab in the same home where his/her child lives."

The Child Endangerment Penal Code is present to protect a child from an abuse that may not leave a physical mark, yet is an abuse of emotional nature. This Penal Code is applicable if a child has suffered an unfounded pain of physical or mental nature, has been willfully caused or permitted to be injured or has been willfully caused or permitted to be placed in a dangerous scenario. Moreover, to apply the charges of this Penal Code, the prosecutor only needs to prove that the child could be physically harmed.

In case of a misdemeanor charge, you are likely to face:

- Six months in county jail

- $1,000 fine

- Informal probation for four years

- One year of child abuser's treatment counseling

- A protective order served against you

In case of a felony charge, you are likely to face:

- Six years in state prison

- $10,000 fine

- Formal probation for four years

- A "strike" in accordance to California's Three Strikes Law

Penal Code 368 pc Elder Abuse

"Penal Code 368 makes it a crime to inflict physical abuse, emotional abuse, neglect, endangerment or financial fraud on a victim 65 years of age or older. The crime is usually charged against caregivers, but can also be charged against anyone who commits these sorts of offenses against a senior citizen victim."

The subject of elder abuse holds a highly sensitive meaning for the citizens, especially in the State of California. With that, there are several cases and a dwelling chance that the individual is wrongly accused of elder abuse based on grave misunderstandings. To avoid wrongful accusation, this law comes into action with its supporting clauses. When a person is accused of elder abuse, he or she is being accused of abuse in terms of physical, emotional, financial fraud or/and endangerment status to a person aged 65 years or older.

If you are proved guilty of committing an elder abuse crime against a person aged 65 years or older, then you will be charged with a misdemeanor or a felony. If the abuse is of physical nature, a misdemeanor is charged. For an elder abuse that is associated with emotional, financial fraud or endangerment, conditions may vary according to the scenario and the previous criminal history of the accused.

Penal Code 422 pc Criminal Threats

"Penal Code 422 makes it a crime to communicate a threat of serious harm to someone if (1) you intend to put the person in fear, and (2) you actually do put the person in sustained fear. Criminal Threats may be charged as a misdemeanor or a felony."

According to this Penal Code, a criminal threat is associated with a person who deliberately threats another individual for inflicting bodily injury. The threat may be in a verbal, electronic or written form. With that, if a person fears for his or her life and feels at risk of harm to themselves or to their immediate family, the charges against the Penal Code of criminal threats apply instantly. The charges against the Penal Code of criminal threats may be of a misdemeanor or a felony, which depends on the previous criminal history of the accused.

If a person is charged with a misdemeanor, they will face:

- One year in county jail

- $1,000 fine

If a person is charged with a felony, they will face:

- Three years in state prison

- $10,000 fine

- A "strike" in accordance to the California Three Strike Law

- 85% of prison sentence must be served before becoming eligible for parole

- If this offense is a defendant's second "strike", he or she will have their prison sentence doubled

- Possible deportation of legal immigrants and aliens as CA Penal Code 422 is a deportable offense

Defending an Innocent

"Domestic violence (DV) is a crime of violence, typically an assault, battery, stalking, or criminal harassment, perpetrated by someone against a family or household member. Some states have specific statutes that are separate from the general assault statutes. In other states, such as California, the prosecutor charges the defendant with general assault or battery, and if the state can prove that the victim was one of the persons considered a "family or household member," the punishment will be enhanced."

What to do if you are falsely accused of domestic violence?

Vincent Imhoff, managing partner of Imhoff & Associates, PC, expresses the need and the way people can use domestic violence laws against their partner and spouse, "It is a way to kick the other spouse out," Imhoff says. "People know how to abuse it [domestic violence accusations] and use it as a tool. They can use a false domestic abuse claim to get someone out of the house. Then the accused has to stay away for 24 hours or until the court date."

"There are several things that go on in making a domestic abuse accusation. First, it is easy to make the accusation. Second, the state has an interest in arresting people for domestic violence because they get federal money per arrest, so they have a vested interest in acting on an accusation that has thin evidence."

Dr. Richard Gelles comments on domestic violence, "Contrary to the claim that women only hit in self-defense, we found that women were as likely to initiate the violence as were men. In order to correct for a possible bias in reporting, we reexamined our data looking only at the self-reports of women. The women reported similar rates of female-to-male violence compared to male-to-female, and women also reported they were as likely to initiate the violence as were men."

Professor John Archer states that, "It has often been claimed that the reason CTS studies have found as many women as men to be physically aggressive is because women are defending themselves against attack. A number of studies have addressed this issue and found that when asked, more women than men report initiating the attack. (Bland & Orn. 1986; DeMaris, 1992; Gryl & Bird. 1989. cited in Straus. 1997) or that the proportions are equivalent in the two sexes (Straus, 1997). Two large-scale studies found that a substantial proportion of both women and men report using physical aggression when the partner did not (Brush, 1990; Straus & Gelles, 1988). This evidence does not support the view that the CTS is only measuring women's self-defense."

With that, a research was conducted on domestic violence that explains, "California State University surveyed 1,000 college women: 30% admitted they assaulted a male partner. Their most common reasons: (1) my partner wasn't listening to me; (2) my partner wasn't being sensitive to my needs; and (3) I wished to gain my partner's attention. Martin Fiebert, Ph.D., Denise Gonzalez, Ph.D., "Why Women Assault; College Women Who Initiate Assaults on their Male Partners and the Reasons Offered for Such Behavior," 1997, Psychological Reports"

- **Getting legal advice**

If you find yourself tangled in a situation in which you believe and are sure that your current or former partner is wrongly accusing you of the domestic violence crime then the best way to start resolving such a critical issue is by hiring a professional and experienced attorney. Once you have an experienced attorney on your side, you can rely on his or her expertise to understand all major and minor realities of the situation and act smartly during the court proceedings. With that, you must remember not to engage in any sort of communication with the law enforcers, in the absence of your professional lawyer. For anything you say or the way you act with those personnel can be used against you in court and cause you to face more serious allegations than previously intended.

Imhoff says, "It takes a lot of gumption for a defendant to want to keep fighting. Often they are worn down by the system or they cannot afford to miss more work. It can be expensive for the defendant so they decide to take a plea agreement."

With that, Imhoff also states that a lot of effort and research are required to make the case strong and favorable for a wrongly accused person, "We look at corroborating evidence—what other evidence is around." Imhoff says. "We look for physical signs of abuse; see if there has been past abuse. We find out if they are in the midst of a divorce and what the witnesses, if there are any, have to say."

- **Meeting your current or former partner (accuser) in the presence of a witness**

If you are going through a split with your partner or spouse, then it is likely that you have to face him or her in face-to-face meetings either for collecting your kids or for picking up your belongings from home. In any scenario, you must be vigilant enough to set up a meeting with your partner or spouse in the presence of a witness. This is because the last thing you need right now is another false accusation of domestic violence or of any other criminal conviction. This could worsen your case and personal position. Hence, meeting your partner or spouse in the presence of a witness is a rational idea and it can definitely avoid such expected instances.

- **Maintain a clear and vigilant mind**

Rationalism is the key to success. Once you are falsely accused of a domestic violence crime, an array of emotions may be going through your mind that could lead to an irrational outlook of things. You must keep your head clear from all possible irrationalities and take logical decisions during the court trial and its proceedings. Your emotion-based behavior or statements could harm you, since they can be used in court and make your case even weaker. Let go of the emotions, stop stressing, and deal with the entire situation with a vigilant mind.

- **Do not act harshly or in a way that could be used against you in court**

Before and during the court proceedings, every action and interaction you get involved in with your spouse and partner should be carefully thought. This is because any unfavorable step you take can be used against you in court. For example, using or threatening with a firearm, joking about suicide or violence, punching walls and showing aggression, or any other action that the court disregards must not be taken up by the wrongly accused individual. Such an action could weaken the already vulnerable case of that individual.

How to defend a person who is falsely accused of domestic violence?

If you are going through a difficult time in your relationship and there is a high chance of a split-up, then you must keenly observe your spouse or partner's behavior. If you notice that your spouse or partner is behaving oddly and hinting at you of accusations such as that of domestic violence (which you believe are unjust and false), then you must consider the following actions. These actions will help you protect yourself against false accusations of domestic violence by being one step ahead of your partner and making their intentions fail in this regard.

- Consult with a domestic violence defense attorney

- Protect your valuables

- Notify family members about your concerns

- Change all of your login information

- If you are the abused, gather evidence

Consequences for the false accuser

If you are being accused by your partner or ex-partner for a domestic violence crime that, in fact, you have not committed, then the accuser has already committed a serious crime by fabricating the reality. For that, the false accuser is likely to serve a number of years in prison if it is proven in court that the allegation was based on a lie.

With that, if the accuser takes the support of falsified information and evidence to prove the case in their favor, they are committing yet another crime. If the case is taken up for a trial in court and you are presented for trial to investigate a crime that you have not committed, then the judge will most likely demand for proof. If they are still lying at this stage, they are committing a perjury. Such allegations and support of fabricated evidence holds serious consequences for the accuser and he or she may have to face a lengthy period in jail if the accusations are proved false in court.

Hence, there are definitive ways in which you can protect and prevent wrong conviction charges on yourself. The key is to hire a professional attorney for yourself that understands such situations and deals rationally by using acquired evidence. Your attorney can help in the court proceedings by smartly identifying whether the evidence against the accused is based on perjury or not. Moreover, once the accuser is proved false, he or she may end up in prison themselves for up to six months or more, depending on the criminal history and the court proceedings.

Chapter 2: The Technicalities

What to Do When it Happens

Different people would deal with a domestic violence issue differently. Some choose not to bring their problem out in the open, while others make sure their abuser is convicted for the crime. When a domestic violence case takes place with you or you suspect someone going through this problem, you must report the incident.

Some people, mainly the abusers, often persuade their victim to avoid going ahead with reporting the crime. They don't want to lose control of the dominance and power they have over their victim in the abusive relationship and want it to continue just the way it is so they can enjoy their supremacy. This is precisely why they make use of different threats to change their victim's mind of bringing the issue in the limelight.

In addition to that, there are some relatives or intimate partners of the victim who fear that they would go through a lot of trouble, if the abuse is reported and ask the victim not to pursue that decision. For instance, sometimes, mothers or current fiancés of women suffering from domestic violence at the hands of their ex-boyfriend or spouse forbid them from reporting the incident, as they don't want to go through the trouble of filing a charge, getting a restraining order, getting an attorney, and going through the laborious trial process. This is an entirely wrong approach to tackling domestic violence. If you know of a domestic abuse or physical assault case, taking place in your area or to someone close to you, you must report it and encourage the victim to report their abuser as well.

Let's take a look at a few important things you should do when you are attacked by an assaulter or are victimized by this trouble.

Don't Attempt to Defend Yourself On Your Own

What do you do when you are informed you have a brain tumor? Do you start cutting your head open to take the monstrous tumor out yourself? Of course, not! You visit an appropriate and qualified doctor who is an expert in treating tumors and get their best advice on what treatment options are most suitable for you.

Similarly, when a domestic abuse case takes place, you must not tackle it yourself. You should not attempt at defending yourself all on your own, neither should you let your family or relatives talk you out of the idea of reporting the incident. The justice system of the country seems like a mystery and misery to all those who aren't familiar with how it can benefit them and the inner sanctum of the system. There are two ways to get everything done: a right and a wrong way. The family facing an allegation and the one being victimized don't know how to correctly approach the justice system. Once a case is reported to the system, it will be taken care of and will be addressed according to its nature. In addition, the state and the system won't drop the case, even if the victim changes their mind about reporting it and want it to be dropped. Once the system becomes aware of the case, it will deal with it.

What Should the Accused Do?

If the domestic violence incident does get reported, the accused must not attempt at saying or doing something to make the case or the accusation go away. The alleged victim cannot do anything to convince and persuade the protectors to stop them from pursuing the case and for making them believe that the abusive incident did not take place. The protectors include the family advocacy center caseworker, advocate of the victim, family advocacy prosecutors, and the police detective appointed in the case.

The accused should bear in mind that the domestic abuse case won't get dismissed till the government of the state believes that the dismissal of the case is in the best interest of the state, not in the victim's or their family's best interest. The protectors only dismiss a case when they have reasonable reason to believe that they can no longer take it ahead or that they will lose it. Hence, if once the case is reported, the accused needs to bear with it and go through the entire process.

The accused needs to get an attorney to represent them in the trial and must always talk in their presence. They must never talk or connect with the protectors, unless and until their attorney is present. Experienced attorneys who are experts in domestic violence know how to tackle the situation best and will guide the accused on how to respond to a certain question or allegation the right way so either the case can get dismissed, or their penalties and charges can get reduced. The accused will have to give videotaped as well as written statements. Additionally, they would have to talk to the prosecutors and detectives on the phone and their calls would be recorded. The accused must maintain their calm and give the right answers so if they are innocent, their innocence can be rightfully proven.

The accused needs to prove that they are innocent and only a skilled lawyer can help them with accomplishing that goal. If the lawyer of the accused and the accused know that they are being falsely accused, then it is important that the false accusation be beaten via an acquittal or a dismissal at a jury trial. If the person is innocent, then pleading guilty will drastically alter their life. If they are not guilty, then they must not plead guilty, as the plea bargain will certainly ruin their life for good. Deferred sentence or adjudication won't result in the conviction of the defendant. If the defendant receives a straight or deferred probation or is released from jail, they will have some criminal record that is normally public.

The defendant would have to go through battering control program and counseling to help them stop their abusive behavior. Make sure your attorney is a qualified one, so they can combat the different tactics of the prosecutor and you do not have to go through unnecessary probation or penalties.

What Should the Victim Do?

The victim of physical and emotional assault first needs to recognize that the assault is taking place. For that, you need to look for signs of domestic violence. Do you often feel scared or are afraid of your partner, boyfriend/girlfriend, spouse or fiancé? Do they constantly assault you, yell at you or make you feel intimidated? Do they blame you for their abusive actions? If you are going through any of these problems, then you are a victim of this problem. Moreover, you should look for all the signs and symptoms of domestic violence that have been explained in the previous chapter. Once you are sure of the crime, taking place with you or someone else in your home, you need to report it right away.

There are different hotlines that you can call on or connect to for reporting the abuse. The numbers and websites of the hotlines are given in the following sections. There is always the option of calling on 911 as well, so make good use of that. You deserve justice and you need to fight for it. After you have reported the crime, you need to begin looking for a seasoned lawyer. Make sure to find one who is an expert on the subject and has fought or dealt with numerous domestic abuse cases. There are a few attorneys, who specialize in fighting and dealing with domestic abuse allegations.

In addition, the victim must understand that they must not back down once they have reported the case. They need to go through with the trials to get their abuser convicted and penalized. If they are honest about their abuse and have actually been subjected to domestic violence, they must not sit silent. Many struggles will come their way and their abuser might try to get in touch with them to emotionally blackmail them and make them change their mind, but the victim must not get intimidated.

For that, it is best that they get a restraining order to prevent their abuser from talking to them. A restraining order is a command issued by the court that prohibits an abuser or accused person from talking, meeting, or getting in touch with the victim. There are various kinds of restraining orders and the victim should go through each one of them to find out which one suits their situation the best. The different types are discussed in the next section.

The Victim

Now comes the part that will help you understand who the real victim of domestic abuse is. 'Victim' means any person, who has been stabbed, assaulted, murdered, abused, or has undergone some type of theft. However, in the eyes of the law, the victim is basically treated as the state. The different criminal cases have their title as 'The State of --- vs. The Defendant'.

Once a crime is reported and the authorities intervene in the crime, they will be intertwined completely with the incident's outcome. The State refers to the prosecutors, the police, and the government and they are solely responsible for deciding if a certain case will either be dismissed or be prosecuted. Even if the person, who is the actual victim, informs the concerned authorities that they want the case to be dismissed, the government itself will make the decision of whether or not to act upon their request. The victim has no power in deciding the fate of their case. However, if the victim's attorney is a qualified and a clever one, they can come up with tactics that will help them accomplish their goal, whatever it may be.

Essentially, the victim is a helpless person who has gone through different kinds of abuse and assault in an abusive relationship. If a person experiences the following then they can be termed as a victim of domestic violence:

- Feel afraid of their partner most of the time, especially when their partner, spouse, boyfriend/girlfriend, fiancé, or parent of their child is at home with them

- Avoid bringing up certain topics, so they don't anger their spouse, partner, fiancé, boyfriend/girlfriend

- Get humiliated or yelled at by their intimate partner or better half

- Get frequently criticized and put down by their intimate partner, fiancé, or spouse

- Feel they cannot do any single thing right or good for their partner

- Are poorly treated by their partner to an extent that they feel embarrassed when meeting their friends, family members, relatives, and acquaintances

- Believe that they deserve to get mistreated or hurt

- Are ignored and cannot voice their opinions and thoughts

- Wonder if they are actually the crazy one

- Get blamed for the abusive behavior practiced by their abuser

- Feel emotionally helpless or numb

- Are seen as a property or sex object by their abuser rather than a living person

- Are often beaten by their abuser

- Are stopped by their abuser from meeting their friends and family or from learning about their rights

- Are restricted by their abuser to access the phone, car or monetary funds, easily

- Are threatened by their abuser that their kids will be taken away from them

- Are forced to do sex or perform other sexual acts by their abuser

- Are always checked on by their partner, spouse, girlfriend/boyfriend or fiancé

- Have their property destroyed by their abuser

In addition to that, you should know that if a person is being stalked by someone, then too, they can be considered as a victim of domestic violence. Stalking is a type of harassment that can make one feel upset or scared. Stalkers can be anyone - someone the victim is familiar with or knows or even a complete stranger. They bother those around them or a particular person by providing them with unwanted attention. It can be in the form of gifts, phone calls, or frequent visits. It can also take the shape of threats. Often people don't regard stalking as a form of a domestic violence, as they state that nobody actually gets physically harmed. However, stalking is a serious issue as it contradicts the law and can turn into physical violence at any point.

Right to Testify

The state of California gives the victims of domestic abuse the right to refuse testimony against their batterer. The crime took place with them so they can decline to testify if they want. However, this doesn't mean that the victims, who decide to hold back their testimony, won't face any consequences after reconsideration or reconciliation.

Before 2009 and the enforcement of the Marsy's Law, the courts in California were authorized to penalize the victims suffering from domestic abuse with community service and jail time if they refused to testify against their batterers. However, due to the enactment of this law, uncooperative victims who refuse testimony against their abusers are only subjected to heavy fines that are affiliated with the contempt of the court as long as they agree to appear during the trial in agreement with the different requirements and regulations of the subpoenas of the victims.

The problem with most of the domestic violence cases is basically the reconciliation shown by the two parties: the abuser and the victim. Once the damages have been paid and the legitimate process has completed its course, the two parties often reconcile with each other. After the victims become fully aware of the troubles their abusers will experience, they decide to change their decision and reconcile with their abuser.

Victims of different domestic abuses might live in co-dependent relationships with their intimate partners. Most of the couples involved in such relationships depend greatly on one another for fulfilling their emotional, financial, and physical needs. It isn't illegitimate to opt for a lifestyle of this sort, but their hard luck is that several other lives become seriously affected by their wrong choices. For instance, the lives of their children, the lives of their parents or of anybody else who lives with them in the same house.

All the domestic violence occurrences aren't similar. Some victims of battery do really want to get out of the miserable life they are living with their abusers. However, mostly they are intimidated or quite uncertain regarding giving testimony in front of the courts when their abusers are present as well. Domestic violence victims are provided with the freedom when they have to decide whether to testify against their batterer. According to paragraph 5, in the California's Victim Bill of Rights 2009: Marsy's Law, it has been stated that people suffering from domestic violence have the right:

- To refuse interview, discovery request or deposition by the attorney of the defendant, the defendant themselves or anybody else acting or speaking on behalf of the defendant

- To set some conditions, according to which any deposition, discovery proceeding or interview should be carried out

Discovery proceedings before the trial takes place aren't exactly same as giving testimony before the jury in court. Abused people do have the right to refuse to take part in any pre-trial discovery, but their refusal is considered unlawful even if that participation isn't worth a lot, still it is considered wise for them to participate in the court and pre-trial proceedings.

The judicial system of the state of California has made attempts for addressing the issue of domestic abuse in different kinds of manners that includes punishing the victims as well if they don't testify against their abusers. However, the problem is again that the lifestyle choices of different people are different and you cannot force someone to act against their wishes. Irrespective of the choice of a victim not to testify, it is considered essential that they look for help offered by a qualified legal representative so they become completely conscious of their rights and the consequences they could suffer from when they refuse to give testimony. It is important to mention that victims of domestic abuse cannot get the legal advice and help of lawyers who are working for their abusers. This goes beyond the ethical line that has been set by the society and could result in malpractice by the attorney. The victims of different domestic abuse might face financial consequences as well when they refuse to testify against their abusers.

Even if the victim refuses to testify in opposition to their abuser, the prosecutor has the right to continue with the prosecution of the defendant. As stated before, the victim is referred to as the state and the state has legal rights to proceed with the prosecution process of the defendant. The decision of the prosecutor to go ahead with the process normally depends on how strong the evidence presented in that case is. Different pieces of evidence include photographs showing the injuries inflicted on the victim such as scratches, marks, black eyes, or bruises and the testimony of witnesses against the abuser such as the close family members, relatives or friends of the victim.

The spouse of the defendant normally won't testify, but the medical professionals and police officers can testify if they had observed any injury on the abuser's spouse or partner. Prosecutors can also go through the criminal record of the defendant, when deciding they should continue with the prosecution of a domestic violence case. The past of the defendant becomes quite relevant when the past convictions pertain to domestic abuse crimes, especially in cases where the prosecutor thinks that the proof of these old crimes has the potential to be presented in front of the jury and the judge.

Domestic violence should never be taken lightly and it can only come to an end when the victims decide to empower themselves with all the rights available to them and become determined to help themselves, as well as others around them who are going through a similar issue. A little courage can help them improve their life for the better.

The Questions You Need to Ask

In the legal books, domestic violence is defined as a behavior pattern that is abusive in nature and practiced by a spouse or partner over the other individual, in order to maintain control over the other partner's actions, life matters, etc. Such behavior is not restricted to beating and hitting only. Here is a behavior breakdown of domestic violence crimes:

- If you have been physically assaulted in terms of being hit, kicked, pushed, spitted, or shoved

- If you have been Intimidated and that makes you fearful for your life

- If you have been threatened in terms of words or actions and to physically assault you

- If you are being stalked, followed or harassed repetitively in a manner that frightens you

- If you are being sexually abused by means of force or coerce

- If you are being deliberately isolated from family, friends or close relations

- If you are being psychologically abused

- If you are being economically abused in a way that interferes your capability of getting or keeping a job or for going to school or controlling money)."

- If you are being emotionally abused

Importance of asking the right questions

When you are a lawyer, you need to ask the right questions to win the case. If you forget to ask the right ones, and ask something that can land you into a pitfall then you can simply lose the entire case.

By considering the case of Crawford and Davis, you can better assess the valuable practice of a lawyer and the way their actions can alter the course of proceedings for a case. "In 2004 the United States Supreme Court issued a decision in Crawford v. Washington that made significant changes in how a prosecutor can use statements from a victim if the victim is not able to testify at a trial. Few victims are in a position to simply walk into a courtroom and say, "This is what happened. This is what he did and how he did it." Such a move could result in far more harmful consequences that may significantly outweigh the value of the help the victim might receive from a conviction.

As a result, many victims do not appear to testify at a trial. While prosecutors can still get a victim's statements to the police and others admitted into evidence and heard by the jury, Crawford made admission of this type of evidence harder. When police officers understand the basic points of Crawford and take care to thoroughly and accurately document statements that occur before an official interview or statement is made, prosecutors are far more likely to get crucial statements admitted into evidence."

The American Bar Association's Commission on Domestic Violence provides the best resource for lawyers who have taken up the domestic violence cases. The Commission's contribution is reviewed as, "Recently, the American Bar Association's Commission on Domestic Violence published a document titled "Standards of Practice for Lawyers Representing Victims of Domestic Violence, Sexual Assault, and Stalking in Civil Protection Order Cases"2 (hereinafter referred to as "ABA Standards of Practice"). I believe that the ABA Standards of Practice is a good reference for lawyers who may choose to represent victims of domestic violence, specifically in civil protection order cases. I will refer to this document whenever applicable; however, the purpose of this article is to provide lawyers with practice suggestions for representing clients who are victims of domestic violence in all types of legal matters, not just civil orders of protections only."

What are the right questions to ask the defendant, witnesses or the victims?

There are many possibilities that can be adopted by the lawyer to screen clients for domestic violence. It is extremely crucial for the lawyer to develop a reliable understanding so that disclosure by the client becomes easier. Here are a few examples of the questions compiled by **American Bar Association Commission on Domestic Violence** in **"Tool for Attorneys to Screen for Domestic Violence"** that you can ask your client in order to screen him or her for domestic violence.

- Has your intimate partner ever hurt or threatened you?

- Has your intimate partner ever pushed, slapped, hit or hurt you in some way?

- Does your intimate partner prevent you from eating or sleeping, or endanger your health in other ways?

- Is there anything that goes on at home that makes you feel afraid?

- Has your intimate partner taken the children without permission, threatened to never let them see you again, or otherwise harmed them?

- Has your intimate partner ever hurt your pets or destroyed your clothing, objects in your home, or something you especially cared?

- Has your intimate partner ever forced you to do something you did not want to do?

When to screen your client, if he or she has been a victim of domestic violence?

If a client approaches you for professional advice on domestic violence, it is not entirely conclusive that the inquirer is in fact a victim of such crimes. The inquirer may be a perpetrator of the domestic violence crimes, who is seeking advice on ways to avoid charges. Furthermore, your client who is seeking for advice may be a victim, but he or she is too ashamed to say it aloud. People hold on to relationships, even though the core of the relationship has evolved into a violent one. Hence, the job of an attorney is highly crucial in this respect since he or she has to raise the right kind of questions that can help identify the precise situation without realization by the inquirer.

How should you react if your client discloses the fact that he or she has been a victim of domestic violence?

Once you have established a fairly mutual communication with your client and your client trusts you enough to reveal that he or she has, in fact, been a victim of domestic violence, you must first assure your client that all information and details being conveyed to your by him or her are held strictly confidential by you. Your client may not trust you at that moment or even later if he or she does not get the surety on confidentiality over what is being discussed with you. With that, you must never advise your client to take a certain action or respond in a certain way. This is not your task to handle and it could lead to severe consequences. Instead, you must advise your client to contact an advocacy, a counselling center, the helpline or the police immediately. They are in a better position to advise your client on what to do next. In addition, assure your client that all conversations with those agencies are also held confidential.

Do you need to be worried about your client's and your own safety from the batterer, once your client has managed to disclose that he or she has been a victim of domestic violence?

Once a victim of domestic violence takes up the courage to report this crime to the authorities, it is likely that the batterer may become more violent than before because of losing power over the spouse or partner. The accused may feel threatened by the accusation and may try to react in a way that could harm the victim even more or even be a danger to your client. In such a case, where the victim has survived domestic violence and wants to report the crime officially, you must prepare your client for all possible threats and security measures to secure their life, finances, assets and other belongings. In addition, your life may also be at risk since you are the prime source of help for your client.

Checklist for ensuring your safety as an attorney of domestic violence case

Here is a precise checklist of the safety measures that must be taken up by you as an attorney of a domestic violence case. This checklist is also compiled by *American Bar Association Commission on Domestic Violence* in *"Tool for Attorneys to Screen for Domestic Violence"*:

- For your safety and that of your client and your staff, safety planning is crucial. Be aware of your own safety. Most batterers seek to control their former or current partners, rather than their lawyers, and many batterers appear to be well behaved in court.

- Yet, batterers and their family members may threaten lawyers for victims of domestic violence. Take precautions if a problem arises. Carefully review your office security procedures.

- If the batterer is representing himself and is coming to your office, do not hesitate to ask a law enforcement officer to sit outside your office or seek similar precautions. You may wish to obtain a protection order that includes the batterer staying away from you and your office.

- Instruct your staff as to how much interaction they should have with a batterer who represents himself and calls your office. All staff should be particularly careful not to reveal last names or personal contact information.

- Find out the safest way to contact your client and the names of other individuals who will know how to reach her.

- Always talk to the client about the case directly and do not leave related messages with family members, friends or other associations.

- If a family member inquires you about your identity, do not disclose that you are a lawyer. Give a generalized explanation about yourself such as presenting yourself as a survey-taker.

- Always ensure with the client that it is safe to converse about the case at that moment. The batterer may or may not be present with the victim at that time so it is always safe to be sure before you talk about the case.

- Make sure your number identification is blocked from being traced.

- Keep your client's location confidential.

- Let your client know that she should not hesitate to call you in the prospect. With that, if your client is not responding to your calls, make indirect efforts to ensure his or her safety.

- If the matter is severe enough and you believe your client's life may be in serious danger, and then call the police immediately.

- Chat with your client in advance about what to do if she vanishes – does she want you to try to find her?

Resources for attorneys who are screening the domestic violence case on behalf of their client

You can find useful data on reliable resources online and from your local telephone directory so that once your client approaches you, you can provide those materials to the potential victims of domestic violence instantly. The most prevalent resources are the local police department, victim witness programs, domestic violence shelters, local domestic violence hotlines and counselling programs. Contact these institutions and request for pamphlets and other literature to keep in your office or waiting room. In this way, you can contribute by providing information to clients in an indirect way. Such information can even save your client from further violence instances and help them protect their life.

In the end, the attorney has a critical and an ethical responsibility to respond in an accurate way to their clients who may be a victim or perpetrator of domestic violence. With that, the entire client-attorney relationship is based on pure confidentiality. The lawyer should advise their client about criminal penalties, the right to appeal, rehearing, modification and other associated details, especially in the case when court proceedings rule out against their favor. It is your responsibility as your client's attorney to assist your client by means of authentic knowledge about procedures and solutions to matters associated with domestic violence crimes and court proceedings. One of the best practices of a professional and experienced attorney is that he or she records everything in writing. In this way, it is easier for you and your client to refer back if ever the case has to be reviewed again.

Domestic Violence and Immigrants

Domestic violence is an enormous and grueling problem for the immigrants living in the U.S. There is a very small percentage of immigrants who inflict domestic violence on their U.S. citizen partners or spouses, but mostly the immigrants living in the country are the ones victimized by this heinous problem.

Both immigrant men and women are subjected to domestic violence, but immigrant women experience this problem more frequently. Immigrant women feel completely trapped in such abusive relationships because of the immigration rules, social isolation, language barriers and shortage of funds. Recently, a study carried out in NYC (New York City) on the issue of immigrant domestic violence, reported that about 51 percent of the victims of intimate-partner homicide cases were born in foreign countries and 45 percent originated from the U.S.

Another study revealed that 48 percent Latinas suffered from increased domestic abuse from the time they had migrated to the U.S. A survey pertinent to immigrant women from Korea discovered that around 60 percent of these women underwent physical abuse inflicted on them by their spouses. It was seen in another research study that 59.5 percent married women - who were immigrants - experienced domestic violence compared to the 49.8 percent unmarried immigrant women. The studies also reported that most of the abusers in the different domestic violence cases used the immigration status of their partner as a means of gaining control over them. In addition, immigrant women tend to suffer more battering, due to their cultural values, than the U.S. citizens do. Most of these women belong to cultures where domestic violence is openly accepted or isn't considered as heinous as other crimes.

Additionally, both immigrant victims and batterers often aren't aware that the social and legal services of the country also apply to them, which is why they continue suffering and inflicting harm, respectively. Battered women do try to flee at times, but they often don't have easy access to the bilingual shelters, food or proper financial assistance. This makes them return to their abuser. Mostly, they also don't get the help of a qualified interpreter during their trial in court, or when reporting a complaint to an operator at 911 or to an officer of the law.

Immigrants are quite vulnerable when it comes to the issue of domestic violence because most of them cannot speak English at all. This causes hindrance in their understanding of the laws and regulations of the country and prevents them from comprehending as well as exercising their rights as immigrants living in the U.S. In addition to that, they are separated from their friends and families, and seldom have someone who looks out for them, living close. This prohibits them from bringing up their problems in the limelight or sharing them with someone who could help them out. Moreover, their abusive partners or spouses are fully aware of their vulnerability, which is why they continue to threat and harm them in numerous ways.

Look at the different ways and techniques used by batterers for harassing their better half or partner to gain complete dominance over them.

- Threats: Abusive partners or spouses who are citizens of the country understand the status of their immigrant counterparts and often use it for threatening them. In case, the victim tries to stand up for their rights or voicing their thoughts, the abusive partner threatens to deport them, or withdraw their petitions for obtaining legal status. This threat is often sufficient to keep them bound in the abusive relationship and forbid them to seek any kind of help.

- Isolation: Batterers often use isolation as a useful tactic for abusing their partners/spouses. They prevent the victim from communicating with their loved ones or their family or relatives back home. In addition to that, they try their best to stop them from learning the English language via any means, so they cannot communicate with the helpful authorities.

- Manipulation Regarding Residency or Citizenship: The abuser also threatens the victim by either not filling their residency papers or withdrawing their application altogether. They also lie that if the victim tried reporting the violence, they would end up losing their residency or citizenship. As the victim does not want to go back due to any reason, they stay quiet and continue to bear all the harms and struggles thrown their way.

- Intimidation: Abusers also make the victims feel intimidated by destroying their legal papers or documents that are required for living in the country. These include resident cards, driver's license, passport and health insurance. When the victims have no legitimate documents that could show them as the residents or immigrants living in the country, they fear they might be deported and drop the idea of reporting their abuse or their abuser.

- Children: If the abuser and victim have children together, the abuser, being the dominant one in the relationship, can use their kids as leverage for gaining complete supremacy over the victim. They threaten that they would take the kids away or even go as far as hurting them, if the victim reported them.

- Economic Abuse: The batterers often go to extreme lengths for preventing their victims from leaving their relationship. They do this by falsely reporting to their employers, that the victims are undocumented and have no right to live in the country, or even get them fired. This makes the victims dependent on their abusers and forces them to continue living with them.

To live a comfortable life in the U.S., the immigrants need to be aware of the following things, so they can quit an abusive relationship.

- Basic Rights: Every person living in the U.S. is entitled to certain rights. These rights are bestowed on them regardless of their legal or immigration status and are given to ensure their fundamental protection in the country. The laws that govern families offer you with the following rights:

  ➢ Right of obtaining a protection order for your kids and yourself

  ➢ Right to get legally separated or divorced from your spouse without their consent

  ➢ Right to get a share in any marital property. If a divorce takes place, the court is responsible for dividing the financial assets or properties shared by the two spouses in that abusive relationship

  ➢ Right to request custody of the kids you have with your abuser and to ask for financial assistance for them. Parents of kids below the age of 21 are normally required to give child support and assistance for children who don't live with them.

  To get these rights or to understand how they work, the victim must seek the help of a professional lawyer. It is best that they try to get in touch with a lawyer who is either their friend or acquaintance and has experience of working with immigrants. In addition to the aforementioned rights, a victim has the right to consult a lawyer whenever they want, to not answer any questions asked by the abuser or their lawyer in case the lawyer of the victim isn't present and the right to defend themselves. It is wise that the victim consults both a criminal lawyer and a qualified immigration lawyer for their case.

- Call Police: Any person suffering from any harm, be they a victim of domestic violence or of any other crime, always has the right of calling the police to get their help. This right is applicable to all the immigrants as well. If an immigrant victim is suffering from any kind of domestic violence, they must get in contact with the police for getting a protection order as soon as possible. They should also call the police if they feel their kids are suffering from their relationship. The police will arrest your abuser if they have reasonable proof of believing that they were involved in domestic violence. You should inform the police of all the abuse that has taken place previously or recently, and should show them your injuries, if there are any.

- Get a Restraining Order: If you have been victimized by domestic violence, you have the complete right of applying for a restraining or a protection order from the court. This order will prevent your abuser from contacting, calling, meeting and hurting you and your kids in any way. In case, the abuser violates the order, you can get the police's help to have them arrested. Applications for filing protection orders can be easily found in police stations, legal and civil service offices, NGOs working for women's rights, women's shelters and courthouses.

- Immigration Options: Immigrants who have fallen prey to domestic violence can file an application for legitimate immigration status in the following three ways:

  ➢ Cancellation of their removal under the VAWA (Violence Against Women Act)

  ➢ Self-petitions to get legal status as per the VAWA

  ➢ U-nonimmigrant status (crime victims)

  To understand these ways, the victim needs to talk to a seasoned immigration lawyer.

- Services Available to the Victims: The victims of domestic abuse in the U.S. can get the help offered by non-governmental or governmental agencies that include interpreters, counseling, emergency housing, monetary help and safety planning. They can get connected with any of the following hotlines given below to get 24-hour free of cost assistance.

  ➢ National Sexual Assault Hotline of the Rape, Abuse and Incest National Network (RAINN) - 1-800-656-HOPE (1-800-656-4673) www.rainn.org

  ➢ The National Center for Victims of Crime - 1-800-FYI-CALL (1-800-394-2255) or 1-800-211-7996 (TTY) www.ncvc.org

  ➢ National Domestic Violence Hotline - 1-800-799-SAFE (1-800-799-7233) or 1-800-787-3224 (TTY) www.ndvh.org

  ➢ National center for Missing and Exploited Children - 1-800-THE-LOST (1-800-843-5678) www.missingkids.com

If the immigrant victims of domestic abuse just try taking a little step forward and get connected to these hotlines or to a good lawyer, they can free themselves from their abusers and live a convenient life in the country too.

The State of California

A domestic abuse conviction in the State of California will penalize the abuser for at least three full years of probation, jail sentence and a complete and certified completion of any 52-week batterer's program that is mandatory for the abuser to attend. This program will require the abuser to attend at least one session of the program every week, for at least two hours. If the abuser successfully completes the two penalties, they will be released from their conviction.

Normally, judges demand convicts of domestic violence to spend at least 30 days in jail, but this isn't something set in stone. Certain judges also allow the defendants to just serve probation, if it is their first offense ever, or if their victim hasn't incurred any substantial injuries. Felony convictions can carry up to a whopping four-year jail sentence. The punishment for a conviction tends to lengthen, in case the defendant has been charged with similar offenses in the last seven years. Injuries suffered by victims that can lead to felony prosecution include broken bones, severe and harsh trauma that results in permanent harm to the brain or body, and wounds that need sutures.

In addition to that, the courts in California are ordered to give a protective command/order to protect the complainant against the criminal threats, violence, sexual and physical abuse, residence exclusion, stalking and other harms inflicted by their abuser. Additionally, the Penal Code section 1203.097 demands the abuser to issue a payment of $400 to the domestic violence organizations and programs.

The District Attorney's (DA's) office normally does not seek any fine, but wants the abuser to go through a 15 to 30-day jail time as a penalty. An alternative for jail time is serving in the sheriff's jail work program known as SWAP. There is an enrollment fee of the SWAP program and serving each day in the program costs around ten dollars. There is another fine known as the victim's fund fine. This statutory fine costs about $100 and the abuser has to pay $200 as the domestic violence fund fine too.

Additionally, the supervision for monthly probation costs around $40/month. There are probation supervision charges, as well as mandatory court security expenses. Defendants can face a jail sentence of around 365 days in the county's jail along with a hefty $2,000 fine. Normally, judges don't impose this tough sentence, but do so in case the defendant goes against the rules and regulations pertinent to their probation period.

Defendants have no right to own guns or any other arms, while they are on probation. If a defendant fails to meet their probation's requirements, they are sentenced to a harsh jail time. Their requirements include undergoing a drug test whenever asked to, getting counseling for anger management, taking substance abuse tests and classes for controlling their abuse. After a defendant begins taking batterer's counseling in a program approved by the court, they can request their judge to cancel the restraining order issued against them to the victim. This can only happen if the victim comes to the court and willingly gives their consent for the cancellation of their abuser's restraining or protection order. If the defendant has been convicted of domestic violence in the past, they are bound to experience harsher penalties.

In case the abuser is an immigrant, being convicted of domestic violence could get them deported from the country, or result in denial of complete naturalization, even if that person is a resident of the country. Conviction of domestic violence is termed as a moral turpitude crime and it can be used for accusation and impeachment in the subsequent prosecutions.

Some abusers experience second thoughts on entering a 'guilty' plea. If they want to take back their plea, they have to make that motion as fast as they can, soon after they have entered the guilty plea. They also need to have a good reason to convince the judge to allow them to take their plea back. There are some reasons that judges might accept, such as that the penalty you will get is actually worse than what you had bargained for when you made the guilty plea. A wrong plea can get withdrawn in case the defendant wasn't aware of any of the conviction's consequences at the point when they plead guilty. The consequence must be serious, like getting deported from the country or losing an important civil right. Grounds such as they're innocent or they have altered your mind regarding the guilty plea, or they aren't ready for taking domestic abuse classes aren't reasonable at all.

Once a defendant gets convicted of domestic abuse, they will be placed on probation and the judge might ask them how well they're performing in their batterer's program. Probationers normally arrive around 8.30am, before the starting time of the court, and then get in touch with the officer of the courtroom probation. If no problem exists, they are provided with a new date and then the defendant leaves before the court begins. In case you arrive early and are asked by the officer to stay, it is most likely that there is some problem and you must not make any statement to the court judge and should get a domestic abuse lawyer to talk on your behalf. This happens mostly when the victim calls to complain about the defendant to the D.A. In this case, you along with your attorney should go over all the evidence filed against you and you should ask them to contact the judge as well.

When a person gets convicted of a domestic abuse crime, they will also have to pay restitution for the hospital bills, numerous years of laborious probation that is supervised by different departments such as the county jail and probation department, and they might also get a prison term that depends on how severely their victim was harmed and injured. If the victim was badly injured then their case will be extremely tough to defend. If they get charged with the felony domestic abuse and violence, they have a monstrous problem at hand. In addition, to get a domestic violence lawyer, they need therapy. They would have to attend the therapy sessions, enroll in a proper program created for controlling domestic violence, attend substance abuse or alcohol control meetings and collect substantial proof that they have attended all these sessions, courses and classes. The better the proof is, the more difference it will make at their sentencing.

The penalty a defendant faces depends a lot on the nature of their case. The California Penal Code 243 (e) (1) is normally known as 'domestic battery' or 'battery'. According to the code, battery is explained as any willful action that has the potential of inflicting injury on another person. The code further defines it as a hurtful and willful act carried out for injuring that person's domestic partner, also referred to as DP. A DP can be a girlfriend/ boyfriend, fiancé, cohabiting partner, spouse or parent of your kid. Harmful activities inflicting injuries can be kicking, punching, grabbing a person's shirt and hitting them. These are referred to as 'low end' activities to inflict injuries, but they can be serious too. This code also states that one has to spend a year in jail and pay a $2,000 fine for these crimes.

The California penal Code 273(d) is slightly different from the first one, as it is pertinent to the abuse inflicted upon children. This code deals mainly with physical harm like a hard slap that leaves a bruise, bruising and fighting a kid, beating a child severely with a hard object or a belt, or hitting the child with any other thing that tends to leave marks on their body. These injuries need to be caused willingly by the abuser for the victim to press charges against them. This code is used for charging the offense as felony or misdemeanor. The charge is dependent on the case's facts and the history of both the victim and the abuser. If the defendant is convicted of misdemeanor, then they will spend 365 days in jail. They will also have to pay a fine of around $6,000. Completing a child's abuse program and getting probation are practical options for defendants working with seasoned attorneys.

The California Penal Code 273.5 is normally known as corporal abuse or spousal abuse. This code is applicable if the supposed abuse took place between two intimate partners like a boyfriend and a girlfriend, or former close partners, spouses, fiancés, or an ex-partner with whom the defendant shares children. Physical injuries inflicted on the victim must be proven properly with reasonable evidence, unlike in the Penal Code 243 (e) (1). In addition, proof should be presented to the judge in the court, if the victim wants to charge the defendant with this code. These domestic abuse cases can be put on trial as felonies or misdemeanor; their punishment depends on the defendant's history as well as on the nature of the injuries incurred by the victim. Misdemeanor conviction tends to result in a jail sentence for a whole year or even probation, if the defendant has a clean record. They can also face a fine of around $6,000. In case, they are convicted of a felony, they would have to do a jail time of around four years.

The California Penal Code 368 is related to elder abuse. It covers physical and emotional abuse, financial abuse, theft and neglect experienced by a victim of domestic violence. A charge following this code can be dealt as felony or misdemeanor. Misdemeanor conviction can result in a jail sentence of maximum one year, with a fine and probation. A felony conviction can result in a jail sentence of maximum four years. The penalty received by the abuser depends on their history as well as on the injuries inflicted on their victim. Defendants with a non-existent or limited criminal record have better chances of having no jail sentence, whereas those with huge records have less chances of getting probation without having any jail time.

What the Victims Can Do?

If a person is being victimized by their partner, spouse, fiancé, boyfriend/ girlfriend, or the other parent of their child, they have a right to get a restraining order against their abuser and file charges against them. A person can get a domestic abuse restraining order, in case someone who has a close and intimate relationship with them threatens or abuse them. It can be either one of the married couple, cohabiting partners, separated/divorced couples, people who dated in the past or are still dating, those who lived or are currently living together, biological parents of a kid, or otherwise closely related people.

If a person's child is facing abuse, then they have a right to file the application for their restraining order on their child's behalf, in order to protect them and other family members from the harms of their kid's abuser.

In case a person fails to qualify for any domestic abuse restraining order, they can request for other orders such as the following:

- Civil Harassment Restraining Order: It can be utilized against roommates, neighbors, distant relatives or coworkers.

- Dependent or elder adult abuse restraining order: It is filed if the victim is a mature, dependent adult, is 65 years old, or falls in the age group of 18 to 64.

- Workplace violence restraining order: It is filed by the employer of an employee, who is suffering from violence or any kind of harassment, inflicted upon them by somebody else.

If they're unsure of what type of order will suit them best, it is best to consult their attorney and discuss their entire situation with them.

When they get a restraining order, their abuser is forbidden to do the following:

- Contact them, come near them, their kids, family members or relatives who live in their home

- Stay far away from their workplace, house and the school their kids go to

- Shift out of the house they share together with the victim

- Keep a gun

- Follow the child visitation and custody orders

- Give full child support

- Pay partner or spousal support

- Pay some specified bills

- Come near their victim's pets

- Alter the insurance policies they share with their victim

- Return or release specified property

- Carry out a substantial activity that would affect their victim's property or harm it, in case the two are married or are cohabiting partners

Once a restraining order is issued by the court, it is entered in CLETS, which is a computer system used all around the state. All the law enforcement authorities and officers have complete access to CLETS. In addition, the restraining order will work everywhere in the U.S. In case, the victim shifts from California to another state, they would need to contact the local police of the new area to inform them of the orders.

One must also know that a domestic abuse restraining order can't do certain things. For instance, it does not end the domestic partnership or marriage the victim has with their abuser, as it isn't a divorce. Additionally, it does not establish paternity of the kids the victim has with the person they have received a restraining order against, unless and until their abuser and they agree to get parentage of their kids and agree that the court should enter a proper judgment regarding the parentage.

The person against whom a restraining order is issued isn't allowed to go and visit certain places. They are prohibited from taking part in certain activities. Moreover, they might be forced to shift out of their home, if they share it with their victim. The order will also affect their ability to visit and spend time with their children. In addition to that, they will also be prohibited to own any gun or firearm and will have to return their existing gun or firearm, and won't be allowed to buy any new ones for the entire duration of the order. The order also affects their immigration status in a certain manner that is better explained by immigration attorneys. In case, the person violates any regulation of the order, they may have to pay a fine, be sentenced to jail, or both.

It is also important to know the different kinds of domestic abuse restraining orders.

- EPO: It stands for Emergency Protective Order and is a kind of order that law enforcement authorities can request for by talking to a judge. Judges are available for issuing EPOs 24/7. Thus, if a police officer answers a domestic abuse call, they can ask any judge they know for an urgent protective order any time of the day. The moment the judge issues the EPO, it comes into effect and its limit can stay for around one week. The abuser can be ordered by the judge to move out of the house they share with the victim and steer clear of them and their kids for seven days. This provides the victim with sufficient time for going to the court for filing a temporary restraining command. For getting orders that last for a longer period than an emergency protective order, one has to file for a TRO (Temporary Restraining Order) that is explained below.

- TRO: TRO is an order that works for a longer time than a simple EPO. When a person visits the court to request for a domestic abuse restraining order, they need to fill out detailed paperwork to inform the judge of everything that took place with them and the reason they want an order. If that judge believes they need protection, they will issue a temporary restraining order to them. TROs normally last for about 20 to 25 days, until the hearing date of the court arrives.

- Permanent Restraining Order: When the victim visits the court to attend the hearing scheduled for their TRO, the court judge can issue them a permanent restraining order. It is not actually permanent as it lasts for up to three years. Once those three years end, they can request another restraining order to keep them safe and sound.

- Stay-Away Order: Also known as the Criminal Protective Order, this order is issued by the authorities of criminal court against the abuser/defendant, during the time their case is being executed in court. If the abuser pleads guilty or is actually guilty, the effect of this order will last for three years after their case ends.

Being aware of the restraining orders and the criminal penalties issued against domestic violence abusers helps people become aware of their rights and the punishments their abusers can suffer from if they decide to bring their story in the limelight.

Conclusion

Domestic violence is a crime and this point cannot be emphasized more. One must understand that this is a crime that is affecting the lives of numerous people worldwide and must be battled with strongly. However, this can only happen when people understand their rights and stop confusing domestic violence with a means to discipline and order people. Although most people think only women are subjected to domestic violence, they must know that nowadays, more men are victimized by domestic violators than women. In the U.S., around 3.2 million men and 1.9 million women suffer from harsh physical abuse on an annual basis.

Moreover, to completely understand what domestic violence is, one must know the difference between the acts that are categorized as domestic violence and those that are not. Some of the acts of domestic violence include pushing your partner in a fight, hitting them harshly, threatening them emotionally, physically, economically or socially, forbidding them to meet their friends or family, making them completely dependent on you for their survival and taking away kids from your spouse or partner. However, holding your partner's, girlfriend's/ boyfriend's or spouse's arm during a fight, shouting at them, arguing with them, or unintentionally pushing them aren't considered as acts of domestic violence.

When you decide to support someone you think is innocent or a victim of domestic violence, you must be aware of the consequences of this support. There could be a good chance that, that person turns out to be the abuser in the end, or someone lying to gain some rights or support from their partner. Moreover, you need to be aware of the different domestic abuse crimes such as the Penal Code 273.5, Penal Code 243 (e) (1), Penal Code 273(d), Penal Code 273(a), Penal Code 368 and penal Code 422. Knowledge of these penal codes helps you know the different kinds of domestic abuse violations and the different penalties issued against each crime.

Before you defend a person, it is your duty to learn everything about them, to ensure you are actually defending an innocent person. Often, domestic abusers are good at hiding their reality and can fake their innocence as well, so you need to be cautious when you choose a client. Moreover, you need to know the importance of asking the right questions at the right time to gain command over your case, so you can help your client win it and get protection from their abuser. Moreover, immigrants living in the U.S. need to know that the country's laws do protect them from abuse/violence and they can always make use of hotlines and shelters for reporting their abuse. Domestic violence can only be stopped once the victims become courageous enough to step out of their cocoon of insecurities and the State of California tries its best to accomplish this goal.

www.ingramcontent.com/pod-product-compliance
Lightning Source LLC
Chambersburg PA
CBHW080615180526
45168CB00007B/2922